THE WORDS
WE PUT
ON OUR
TOMBSTONES

Leanne Ayse

TRIGGER WARNING

This story portrays the night of a crisis from the point of view of someone with mental illness. Reader discretion is advised. If you or someone you love needs helps, please reach out. There are resources available for you. The national suicide and crisis lifeline can be reached by calling 988, they are open twenty four, seven and in my experience the counselors are very nice. Please don't hesitate to call them if you need them.

LEANNE ALYSE

To everyone who held my hand and walked
through the darkness with me

LEANNE ALYSE

PLAYLIST

Viva La Vida – Coldplay

I'll Follow You into the Dark – Death Cab for Cutie

Death Bed (Coffee for Your Head) – Powfu

I Hate It Here – Taylor Swift

Fireflies – Owl City

Break My Heart Myself – Bebe Rexha ft. Travis Barker

when the party's over – Billie Eilish

I SHOULD CALL HER

Feeling like you don't exist causes all sorts of problems. What's the meaning of life if you can't even rationalize that life is actually happening around you? My husband sits behind me rubbing my back as the phone trills ringing 988. I've called crisis lines in the past but they never actually connected me to anyone. I don't have much hope for tonight.

"You're okay." He whispers.

I don't believe him. All I can do is try not to stare at the black void man standing in the shower. The man tall as my ceiling who's staring at me. Why is he staring at me?

He wants to hurt me.

Everyone wants to hurt me.

I feel so raw.

It's the middle of the night and the lights are off in our bedroom. The TV is playing The Office, but the screen is set to have the power off. Our bedroom opens up into our bathroom and every time I pull my eyes away from the shower the man reappears.

Maybe if I just stare at it he'll go away.

I glance over and the figure is gone. I think I'm safe so I look back down at the phone trilling and then he's back so I look at him again.

Yeah, that's not helping.

I feel like a crazy person.

"A counselor will be with you as soon as possible. Please stay on the line. Some relaxing music will play as you wait." The automated voice says.

"You're okay." My husband keeps rubbing my back.

I don't need the hold music; there is too much going on right now. Between the TV playing, that stupid catchy new pop song playing in my head over and over again, and the screams ringing in my ears; the last thing I need is more noise. But the hold music doesn't play long.

"Thank you for reaching out." The woman with the overly soothing voice says. "There is always help here when you need it. What's going on?"

She doesn't ask for my name like I was expecting, not that I can remember my name right now anyways. She doesn't ask for my location. She doesn't even tell me her own name. She just waits for me to respond.

"I don't feel real." I whisper through soft sobs, just letting myself exist as best I can. I'm not sure I want to exist right now. I don't want to die; I'm scared to die, but I don't want to exist either. I don't feel like I do.

My tuxedo cat comes and rubs his face up against the phone and I shoo him away even though a part of me wants to just snuggle with him and cry more. I don't remember his name right now either.

"That's an understandable feeling." The woman lilts softly like a smooth jazz singer. "Is this something you feel a lot?"

I nod even though she can't see it. "Yeah. I've mentioned it to my therapist once before and we touched on it for a second."

"When you say you 'touched on it for a second.' What do you mean by that?" The woman asks. Her tone is so even and I can't tell if that's soothing or scaring me.

"She coached me on some grounding techniques and recommended I try to refocus on the present." I had tried those ground techniques before I called and none of them worked. I tried naming everything I saw. I tried counting random objects. I tried focusing on my breathing. Nothing made me feel anymore real.

My brain can't feel my husband rubbing my back anymore but I know he is. I feel him blend into the background like the bed I'm sitting on, the blanket on my lap, everything but the noise.

There's so much noise.

I don't feel connected to my body. Real life feels like playing a video game where I know my consciousness isn't actually in the character. Where I feel like I'm hovering above my body but I'm not in it.

"Do you think maybe she was trying to give you some coping techniques so you could work through how you're feeling in the moment, but it's something you'll dive deeper on further in therapy?" The woman asks.

I shake my head. "I... I don't know." I don't feel like I know anything right now. I'm not sure I'll ever know anything ever again.

I take a deep breath trying to calm myself down. I can feel my body racing, my heart pounding from the panic attack. But I don't feel panicked, I feel scared but... calm; just empty.

"That's okay." The woman says.

I look to my husband expecting him to say something but he doesn't. He just keeps trying to comfort me while I talk to the woman with a scared look on his face; one full of concern for his wife and a helplessness knowing he can't save her from herself.

Glancing down I notice my shirt. Well, not mine, my husband's. It's the same shirt I've slept in for the past three nights... maybe more. I don't know anymore; time doesn't feel real. I don't feel real.

I need to breathe. That's what I was trying to focus on right?

"Maybe your therapist was waiting for you to feel a little better so you could dive into how you're feeling?" The woman on the phone, whose name I still don't know, suggests.

I sob softly again, rubbing away the tears from my red eyes. "I don't know." I whisper again. Everything on a loop. Everything not real.

"That's okay." The woman offers, trying to console me.

"I'm scared." I mutter quietly, but loud enough that I think the phone picks it up. "I was feeling better earlier." I turn my head down feeling ashamed of that I don't feel okay now.

"When you say earlier do you mean a few days ago? Or earlier today?" She asks.

"I felt okay earlier today," I clarify. "But I haven't felt good since I got off my old meds." I run my hands over the soft side of my blanket. "They... they had me on an antipsychotic but... they took me off of it and put me on a ummm...". I pause trying to remember what the new class of medication is called. It takes me a second and I almost consider giving up and abandoning the sentence entirely but then I remember. "A mood stabilizer."

Complex sentences are hard right now. Anything that's a mix of a thought, that's more than the basic; I can't process. I've been struggling with this for days. Over the past two weeks since I got off my old meds and onto the new ones I have had many episodes like this, but this one is one of the worst.

It had been years since my condition was this bad. I had been on the antipsychotic for a long time and it was helping but the weight gain became a concern. Weight is always a concern. But I don't tell that to the woman on the phone.

I just need to get through the night.

"So it sounds like you have a care team. That's good." The woman's voice sounds like she smiles a little. I wonder how many calls like this have favorable outcomes. I wonder how often she hears someone die on the phone with her. Someone she can't save.

"Yeah." I murmur.

A silence passes.

"Have you hurt yourself?" She asks, nerves in her perfectly pleasant voice showing for just the briefest moment.

"No." I reply.

The relief in her voice is clear. "Have you thought about hurting yourself?" She asks, the nerves still there but less prevalent.

"Yes." I answer honestly, even if I don't want to. I've spent so long hiding how bad my mental state was from professionals, not wanting to get committed, not wanting them to think I'm crazy. But in that moment I know I need help and I opt for truth over the mask I usually slip on.

My chest feels heavy and I can't tell if my heart is beating. I'm sure it is, I would know if it wasn't, but I can't tell.

"Do you think about it often?"

"Yes." I feel my husband's hand pause for a second on my back before going back to rubbing it softly. "But I'm safe." I rush out. "My husband is here and I have him and..." I stop before I talk her out of helping me.

"Have you discussed these feelings with your therapist?" I wonder what she looks like. The anonymous woman who's just a voice on the other end of the line. Is she even real?

I sniffle. "Not really."

"Maybe it would help if you talked to her." She suggests.

I nod. "Yeah."

There is another pause on the line.

"Do you want to keep talking?"

I play with my fingers, folding them to-gether and touching each one with my thumbs. "Yeah."

"What would you like to talk about?" She asks softly. She doesn't sound impatient or demanding, just like she's trying to let me lead the conversation so I can say what I need to.

On the plus side this has distracted me from the man in the shower. I look down at my older beagle laying out on the floor beside the bed. He glances up at me and gives me a smile like he's trying to help too.

"I'm scared." I tell her.

"That's okay." She promises. "Have you tried any of the grounding techniques?"

I nod and quickly realize she can't see that. "Yeah... Yeah... they aren't... really helping."

"Is there anything that does help when you feel like this?"

"Sometimes it helps if I sit outside, but it's night time and I'm scared." What if something is out there in the darkness. My mind starts conjuring images of twenty foot wolves, of a man holding a gun, of dying.

The woman hums like she's trying to think. "Do you have any plants in your house or your apartment?"

I look to my husband and he shakes his head. "No." I tell her.

"Maybe can you open a window?" She tries again, her voice full of optimism that this window opening idea will be the magical solution to fix all my life's problems.

"I..." I don't want to disappoint her, but I don't really want to open a window for the same reasons I don't want to go outside. "I could go sit on the porch. Our porch locks and it's screened in." It's the best compromise I can give her.

"That sounds like a good idea." She smiles. "Do you want to go do that?"

Not really, but it might help and I'm willing to try anything at this point. "Yeah."

"Do you want to keep talking?"

"No. I'm okay. I think I'm going to go sit outside." I answer, not feeling very confident that this is actually going to help.

"Are you going to be okay?" She asks.

I look at my husband. "Yeah, I have some-one here." I reassure her.

"You can always call back if you need." She promises me. "We are here twenty four, seven. Thank you for calling in and I hope this helped."

I nod. "It did."

"Goodbye." She says.

As I hang up the call, I can't help but think about that I probably will never speak to that woman again. I wonder how many people in my life I've already spoken to for the last time.

THE GREAT OUTDOORS

"**D**o you want to go outside?" My husband asks, speaking for the first time since the phone call. He hasn't stopped rubbing my back.

I push up off the bed. "Yeah let me pee and put on some pants." I nod softly, more to myself than to him as I get up. I feel his eyes watching after me as I head into the bathroom, like he's wanting to make sure I'm safe.

I feel no relief as I empty my bladder, only anxiety as I imagine myself touching the electrical socket when I go to wash my hands. I need to get those child proof covers for them. Am I really no better than a toddler? I'm twenty fucking four. I feel pathetic. I feel empty.

I finish using the bathroom, flushing the toilet and pulling my panties back up quickly. As I go over to the counter I squeeze some of the soap into my hands and stare at the sink forebodingly like it's going to reach out and smack me.

I can't do this.

I'm convinced I will reach over and touch the outlet. I'm convinced the despair will take hold for a brief moment and I will give into the temptation and let myself get hurt. So I turn around and march out of the bathroom down the hallway towards the kitchen. I can wash my hands somewhere else.

"Where are you going?" My husband asks, confused.

"To wash my hands in the kitchen." I answer like that's the most normal thing in the whole fucking world. I don't wait for him to say anything else before walking over to the stainless steel sink and turning it on.

I glance down at the garbage disposal as I wash my hands and for a brief second get scared that maybe it would somehow be able to electrocute me too. I know that's not how garbage disposals work... well I know that in my rational mind, but the rational mind has long since fled tonight, leaving behind nothing but the id and the id says stick your hand down your garbage disposal and turn it on.

I quickly pull my half soapy hands out of the water, deciding that it was close enough to clean, and wipe them off on the kitchen towel.

My husband is standing in the door to our bedroom watching me as I head back towards him. "I thought you wanted to go outside?"

I nod. "I need pants." I answer, going back into the bedroom and slipping on some pajama bottoms. I don't know how many days in a row I've worn these either. A lot. I wonder when the last time I showered was. Probably when I dyed my hair.

15

My husband holds out a hand to me and I take it letting him guide me through the house and out to our back porch.

Our younger beagle follows closely behind, so close it's like he's trying to trip us. I don't think he understands what's going on. I think he just is excited to go frolic around outside. He doesn't know mommy is having a crisis.

My husband scolds our dog, calling him by his name and telling him to calm down, but the dog doesn't understand and just excitedly hops through the back door. I open the porch door, letting the pup out into the backyard, and he starts to sniff at the grass.

I lock the door behind him quickly, scared that someone is going to try to break in and hurt me if I don't close it fast enough. There is a light outside shining on the backyard, but it still feels dark. I don't like the dark.

I stare out at the backyard for a minute, waiting for something to pop out or for my mind to start conjuring up shapes in the blank spots, but nothing happens.

My husband comes up behind me and guides me back onto the couch on the porch. He stands beside me as I sit down and continue to watch the inky night, waiting for it to move.

It's so quiet.

Our dog walks around outside carefree in a world that is full of nothing but bones and tummy scratches while I sit here burdened with the concepts of reality. While I confront my mortality and my sense of self seems to dissolve into nothing.

My husband pets my head gently, standing over me like a watchful guard, but is he protecting me or keeping me trapped here I don't know. He wants what's best for me... I know that, maybe more than I want what's best for me. Logically I know that.

Screaming rings from behind my eyes and I reach up to cover my ears against it but it's not coming from out there, it's coming from in here. I cringe as I try to take some more stupid breaths, just wanting the droning to stop. "Help." I whisper softly, or at least I think it's softly, I can't really tell over the screaming.

"I'm here, baby." He promises. "I've got you."

I want his words to be a comfort but they just sort of fade into the background of the screaming. They don't feel real. I don't feel real.

Our dog comes to the door and my husband lets him back inside the house to leave the two of us alone to process my bullshit. He positions himself at the window to the back door so he can look out because even if he doesn't know something is wrong, he knows he needs mom.

My husband sits down on the couch next to me and pulls me into his chest. I hear his heartbeat and take a shaking breath trying to calm myself down. He keeps stroking my hair as I try desperately to scrape together the shards of my existence into some form of a functioning person.

"How did I get here?" I whisper, sitting upright and staring out at the still backyard.

I watch the trees sway in the cool fall night air. The leaves have not yet began to fall from the trees but the weather has started to chill.

My husband turns to look at me. "Like how did you get outside?"

I shake my head and my mind drifts back over the history of our relationship. I remember our wedding, I remember the first day we met, I remember a bunch of other little moments in between... and none of them feel real. Did any of those actually happen? Or are they just someone else's memories I'm holding. A past version of myself who's no longer real, who just existed in that moment.

"How did I get here?" I say again, not really expecting an answer.

"What do you mean?" He asks, gently.

I chew on my lip. "Like, how did I become this person? Who am I?"

He tells me my name. "You're a writer. You're a baker. You're a hairstylist. Loving

LEANNE ALYSE

wife. Caring daughter. Great sister." That's
what it will say on my tombstone.

I start crying again.

I don't want to die.

My husband shushes me. "You're okay."
He promises, pulling me back into him.
"You're okay, baby."

"How did I become this person?" I ask
again. "Why did I choose to be any of those
things?"

"Because they make you happy." He answers. "You like baking, and doing hair, and
writing."

I just keep crying into his shoulder. I don't
know if any of those things make me happy.
Actually as a matter of fact I'm sure one of
those things don't anymore. I don't know
what makes me happy. Does this relationship make me happy?

Who is he?

Why did I choose to be with him? Why
did he choose to be with me? I don't voice
that though, I'm scared he'll tell me he
doesn't want to be with me.

He rubs my back gently and keeps shushing me, keeps telling me that I'll be okay but after a while it stops working.

I pull away from him and go back to staring at the bushes and the trees, is something going to pop out? Is something coming for me?

My heart is pounding loud in my chest and I'm scared I'm going to have a heart attack. I force myself back to my breathing exercises. Force myself back to some semblance of sanity, but then everything just starts to become quiet. Too quiet.

I shake, sitting silently and starting to dissociate. I can't feel my body. I can't feel my mind. I can't feel anything. Everything goes numb as my brain starts to make one of its last ditch efforts to try and protect me.

"Baby." My husband whispers softly, but I don't hear him, I don't respond. I just keep staring, unblinking, unmoving, unfeeling, just staring.

ALL THAT GLITTERS

"**C**an we go back inside?"

"Yeah." My husband responds, helping me to my feet and guiding me back towards the house. He goes to lead me back to the bedroom, but I stop in the living room and sit down on the couch. "Did you want to go lay back down?"

I shake my head.

The bedroom has been where I've been having a lot of my anxiety. I feel like I need a change of scenery. Just somewhere else to be for a little while. Somewhere that's not going to cause a pavlovian fear response.

"Okay." He moves one of the blankets we keep on the couch and sits down next to me.

I stare down at the hexagonal shapes on the carpet, I remember having counted them one day trying to use it to calm my anxiety... it worked that time. It won't this time.

I pull my phone out of my pocket and look at the call log. There are a lot to my mom, a few to my brother, some to my husband, and the most recent one sitting at the top of the list to 988.

"I think I need to call them back." I whisper.

"Okay." My husband agrees. He waits for me to hit the number, and my finger hovers over it for a second but I don't press down.

"I'm scared."

Our younger dog walks past and my husband watches him. Then his eyes drift to the unlit fireplace in the center of the wall. "You know what I don't understand?"

"Hmm?" I ask, looking up at him.

"Well, the fireplace vents to the outside to let the smoke out of it, but why does rain never come in through the fireplace?" He asks, likely not expecting an answer from someone in such a catatonic state, but I have one.

"There is a little cover that goes over the top, it has almost like a roof over it with vents to let the smoke out." I sniffle, my eyes darting around the room frantically, looking for my own answers that I will never find.

I turn off my phone and place it on my fingers, holding it up to show an example of how the air flow works. "See so it comes out the sides."

"Oh, that makes sense." He leans in to kiss my forehead. "Thank you, baby."

I nod and go back to staring at the call log. Go back to considering if I should call the crisis line again, but then my mind starts to drift to my parents. I think about how my dad always knows lots of random cool stuff and how that moment of distraction was the most relief I have gotten all night.

"I think I want to call my parents." I tell my husband.

He nods. "Okay."

I press my mom's name and the phone starts to trill again. It takes a few rings but then the line picks up.

"Are you okay?" She asks immediately. It's too late for just a social call.

"I dunno." I sniffle.

"What's wrong?" My mom asks.

I shake my head. "I... I don't know."

"Is it the medicine?" She asks.

I'm starting to get overwhelmed by the questions. My anxiety spikes a little higher not knowing how to explain to her that I don't really feel like a real person right now. I love my mom, but I just... I don't think she would understand that feeling. I think she would try to say something helpful, but her version of helpful is trying to fix things and I can't fix this. I don't want to let her down.

"Is dad there?" I wipe at my eyes.

"Yeah, nene, I'm here." He answers softly.

My mom tries to help more, but her version of help is more questions I can't answer. "Did you take the medicine they prescribed you earlier today?"

"No."

"Why not?" She asks.

"I'm waiting til tomorrow so I can take that at the same time as the other one." I try to explain. They are moving my one medication to a night time dose and starting me back on my old antipsychotic. It makes the most sense to just wait and take both tomorrow.

"I think you should take it now." She advises, and I know she's just trying to help, but I also don't think she understands that it feels like she's pressuring me to do something I don't want. "The old medication helped you right?"

"Yeah, but–"

She just keeps going. "I really think you should take it.

"Is dad still there?" I ask again.

"Yeah, I'm still here." My dad says.

I nod and the line is quiet for a second. "Can you tell me a random cool fact?"

"A random pool fact?" He asks, confused.

I shake my head. "A random cool fact." I clarify, spelling out the word. "Like you know a lot of cool stuff, what's something cool you know?"

My dad hums over the phone thinking on it for a second. "Semi trucks are fifty three feet long." He says, with a shrug in his voice.

"That's cool." I respond.

"Yeah. They used to be forty feet, but they changed it." He explains. "And they are usually eight feet in width."

"How big is the average road?" I ask.

"Depends. Average is probably about ten, the highways are bigger though. Those usually are closer to twelve because you're going at such fast speeds you need more buffer room."

I stare back at the random hexagons on the carpet. "That makes sense." I shake my leg trying to calm myself down, trying to relieve some of the energy. "What else?"

My dad thinks for another moment. "Silver always used to be traded at sixteen to one with gold. And copper was traded at sixteen to one with silver. It was like that for thousands of years for as long as they've had gold, silver, and copper, up until the nineteen hundreds."

"Why sixteen to one?"

"Because that was the ratio of it in the earth's crust." He answers.

"That makes sense."

My dad laughs. "No, it doesn't. They didn't have the technology we have today. How did they know the ratio of what was in the earth's crust back then? They were just guessing."

I chuckle a little.

"Now silver and gold are traded at eight one to one." He scoffs at the high numbers.

"That's crazy."

"Yes. Yes it is." My dad agrees.

"Hey, nenes?" My mom chimes in. "If I tell you not to think of a purple elephant. What do you think of?"

"A purple elephant." I answer.

"Brown zebra." My husband smiles.

"Right." My mom says. "It's all about training your brain to focus on something else. If you try not to think about it you will think about it but if you focus on something else, your mind will think about that."

I nod. "Yeah."

"Are you feeling better?" My mom asks.

"Yeah." I tell her. "I'm doing okay."

"Try and get some sleep, okay?" She says softly.

I nod. "Yeah. I will. Love you guys." My mom, dad, and husband all say love you back and I hang up the phone.

"Are you feeling any better?" My husband asks.

I nod. "Yeah." I tell him. "That helped."

"Do you want to try and get some sleep?"

I nod. "Yeah."

Acknowledgments

I'm gonna keep this short and sweet because of how short the story was.

Thank you to the crisis worker who took my call.

Thank you to the people who sensitivity read this because it definitely needed it.

Thank you to my husband and my parents for talking to me and helping me get through the night.

Thank you to all the authors who came before me and inspired my works. Nothing is ever original and I'm okay with that. Where have I heard that before?

As always, thank you to typos. Withoot you I would be nothing. You make me the author I am today and I love you.

Finally, I want to thank God, because God gave me this book, and I feel God in this Chili's tonight.

ABOUT THE AUTHOR

I'm bad at talking about myself but can write a 500 page book about someone else. Do with that information what you will.

As a kid I dreamed of being an author. I took a creative writing class in high school then proceeded to go on with my life and do nothing with it. That was until one day I decided to open a silly little document and start writing a silly little story about a healer and two kings who were in love with her. That cute little pet project that I thought would just be scrapped ten chapters in turned into a full blown trilogy that I'm more proud of than I can even explain.

I've always been a dreamer and sometimes if you keep your head in the clouds long enough, you do actually touch the stars.

I got married in September of 2024 to my loving husband. We had been together 4 years at that point and he's always encouraged me to go after what I'm passionate in. Finding that person who helps you achieve is so important and it's the best quality trait I could ask for in a partner.

Thanks for spending your time to read this. I hope you're having a great day and please make sure to check out my works. There's always more coming out. I'm one of those people who always has to be working on something so I promise you I am.

CHECK OUT MY OTHER WORKS

<u>The Asher Series</u>
    Asher
    Burned
    Change

<u>A Literal Series Name</u>
A Cozy Airport Read

CHECK OUT MY SOCIALS

Tiktok: @84Lele

Instagram: @the84Lele

Twitter: @84Lele84Lele

YouTube: @84Lele

www.ingramcontent.com/pod-product-compliance
Lightning Source LLC
Chambersburg PA
CBHW050909120626
46554CB00003B/1092